GW00733346

A Little Book
Of Sport Stories

Jo Gunston

Published by Sports Liberated
www.sportsliberated.com

Cover design by Jason Keens
Initial critique by Jacky Gunston

DEDICATION

For Jason, although I know you'll be too mortified to actually read this.

Also, big love to Max, Pax, Caroline, Ali, Charlie, Lucy & Milly.

CONTENTS

Jo Gunston

ACKNOWLEDGEMENTS

Part of my love of sport is the enjoyment of meeting so many different people on my travels, however, they may not always want to be featured in a book of my short stories. If I believe someone is happy to be featured in these pages I name them, if not, I use nicknames or fudge a way around it. All of these stories are true. Some minor details may differ from how the other people involved remember them – that's just true of any real-life story.

I make no apology for making up my own words throughout.

You are already donating to children's cancer charity Amelie's Rainbow by buying this book as five per cent of profits will be donated to the fund. If you can help further, however, please head to the following Go Fund Me link where 10-year-old Amelie is trying to raise as much as she can to help other kids in the same position as her following her own diagnosis. Thank you from Glen, Lisa, Hugo and Amelie.

www.gofundme.com/amelies-rainbow

1

THAT TIME I WAS IN
THE LONDON 2012
OPENING CEREMONY

Should you ever find yourself heading to your first audition may I suggest not washing your trainers the night before and leaving them out to dry? They don't dry so quick.

One Sunday morning in November 2011, eight months before the start of the London 2012 Olympic Games, I find myself squelching along the odious back streets of east London. I'm heading to an audition that will hopefully result in me taking part in one of the ceremonies that will bookend the Olympic and Paralympic Games.

Since July 2005, when London had won the right to stage the iconic global sporting event, I'd subscribed to any and every email to do with my hometown Games. When an email pings through calling for volunteers to audition for ceremony parts, I'm on it like a rash.

Cursing the loss of my recently dispatched Fame-inspired leg warmers in a declutter-your-life-inspired frenzy, I dress in tracky bums, artfully distressed Atlanta 1996 Olympics motifed T-shirt and the aforementioned damp trainers.

The auditions of nigh on 10,000 people are set to take place at 3 Mills Studios, 'London's largest film and television production studios', and a mere five miles from where I live.

The capital offers its very best in convoluted ways to get to my nearby destination. Ongoing Tube works? Tick. Car park facilities at the venue unavailable to auditionees? Tick. Fourteen different buses to get there? Tick.

So, on this drizzly grey morning, my boyfriend Jason drops me off as near as he can to the venue, ready for my 9am start. I still have to make my way through a graffiti-daubed tunnel, past a rotting mattress and through a gas leak haze, but then voilà, I'm there.

Sizing up

Clutching my passport, I join a line that snakes around a warehouse-style building and get chatting to those around me. A middle-aged artist nervous and flighty as a bird: "Am I wearing the right shoes? The wrong shoes? What do you think? I'm going to change them. No, I'll keep these on. Can you hold these, please?"

I bond with a woman even more petite than my 5ft-2ins and we fill the waiting time discussing potential costumes. Perhaps we'll be a mushroom or a flower we ponder, our lack of performance experience clear in our primary school drama-inspired musings.

Once inside and through security photos are taken for our passes 'in case we get through'. Even at this early stage we're also measured for costumes.

I'm intrigued by my measurement of seven inches for my hands and amused by one figure in the next numbers.

"32ins."

Yep, knew that.

"24ins."

Get me with my little waist.

"38ins."

What? My butt is 38 inches. Are you kidding me? I won't need those butt implant thingies, then.

Once inside, the guy who has had the masochistic 'pleasure' of organising the ceremonies for the past four Olympic Games addresses us. Trying to get a handle on the sort of volunteers he has in front of him he asks various questions as we excitedly gather around him.

Have any of us gone to any previous Olympics, he asks, and if so, what memories do we have? Usually one to spout my sport superfan credentials at any opportunity I find myself tongue-tied. I can only think of being robbed on the train on the way to the stadium at the Athens Olympics, which seems a tad negative, so I keep silent in case a cross is marked against my name.

One fella has flown in from Philadelphia for the audition, trumping everyone with his enthusiasm. The director of operations points out the American's thin, well-worn T-shirt. "Yes, it's from the 1996 Atlanta Olympics," the man explains proudly. "I was a volunteer there, too."

I cross my arms over my own Atlanta 1996 motifed top, as I clearly can't compete with this man's devotion. My trendily distressed top was bought the previous week from Next.

Marching to a different drum

The next three hours can only be described as a 'drill'. We walk, march and jog along lines taped to the floor, school-gym stylee. Music pumps out beats and clipboard-laden staff mingle among us, scratching down notes after peering at the number pinned to our clothes.

We're separated into big groups, small groups, directed to one side of the area, to the back area, nothing complicated, just following instructions. I'm a former gymnast so very much used to being coached and I do everything exactly as asked. Except one thing.

At one point we're told to stay in line, to follow the markings on the floor but "do your own thing". I act on this with gusto, dancing up a storm to the music, but within this melee I don't hear the next instruction, something that has consequences in what happens at the next audition. That's right, I said next audition, I make it through the first hurdle.

Out of step

"You have been selected," says the head honcho of the ceremonies cast, "because you all did your own thing during the first audition. You're now all auditioning for the main dance in the Olympic Games opening ceremony."

Gulp.

The reason I've been chatting to professional dancers all morning suddenly becomes all too clear. I am in over my head.

Not only that but the previous day I'd had a cortisone pain-killing injection in my spine due to an old gymnastics injury so this is me 'resting' after the procedure.

We stand in a grid formation and I'm next to a guy with three giant purple spikes jutting out of his black slicked-down hair. A professional dancer (natch) he's just arrived having danced on a nightclub podium until dawn.

Yours truly, meanwhile, had an early night, fuelled up on energy-giving carbs for dinner, and has bananas in her bag, plus plenty of liquid to keep hydrated throughout the day. As we stand on our grid positions, the instructor points out my spiky-haired friend.

"You with the hair. You're a good point of reference for everyone else. When we ask you to get back to your grid positions you'd better make sure you know where your position is. I want you to be the marker for everyone else."

This makes my life easier, I think. Turns out, finding my grid position is the only thing that's easy that day. We start off with a few steps. Bam, bam, turn, turn, boom diddy boom and cha. And again. "Feel free to add your own interpretation," we're told.

"Okay, let's move on and add some more steps. Da da daaaa, step step, twist, step, dum dum. Let's go. Great. Right, let's add the two together. Perfect. Okay, and next section..."

And so it goes on, with more mini steps added to the previous sections. I start well but get increasingly confused the more moves are added to the routine. It's possible this is where being a professional dancer is an advantage.

A few hours in and I'm forgetting how the dance even starts but decide to brazen it out, grinning inanely and adding personal touches to my incorrect steps. Those audition stalwarts around me execute the routines flawlessly adding their own flourishes for extra oomph.

By the end of the audition I feel deflated, I'm so clearly out of my depth I must have blown my opportunity. I had enjoyed my Flashdance-plus-200-people moment but I'm gutted but not entirely surprised when a few days later I receive an email saying, 'Thank you for your time but at this point you're a reserve'.

Friends and family say I've done well to get this far. I nod but I'm never going to be satisfied with that.

Never, ever give up

In May 2012, two months before the Games begin I'm still just a reserve – I have to do something.

My feverish desire to be part of the London Olympics stems from a career-curtailing back injury, suffered during my teens, from my beloved gymnastics. London, therefore, is my Olympics, the Games I never made.

Like many fans, I've applied for a gazillion tickets via a ballot system and also been interviewed for a Games Maker role – basically a volunteer – yet so far I've ended up with nothing. So I do what anyone would do. I write casting a poem. Along the lines of 'I live down the road, in the Olympic post code' I use the term 'poem' loosely.

A plea to whoever receives this ode
From a reserve left by the side of the road
Please know that I am here
Waiting for the all clear
I even live in the Olympic postcode.

The opening ceremony is what I await
My schedule is a clean slate
Two auditions I did complete
Tip tapping my dancing feet
But now I await my Olympic fate.

So to you I do ask
Let me help with your task
To welcome the world to our host nation
Going above and beyond expectation
To help inspire a generation.

Two days later I receive a phone call from casting.
"We love your poem," they say.
"It was rubbish," I blush.
"You're in," they conclude.
"Waaaaaaaaaaarrrgggggghhhhhh," say I.

My own rhapsody

Most cast members have been rehearsing for up to 10 hours a day for the previous six months at this stage but my late entry, along with nine other lucky souls, comes about because of opening ceremony head honcho Danny Boyle.

The London-based director, known for films such as Slumdog Millionaire and Trainspotting, wants to emulate the hologram effect in Queen's music video for Bohemian Rhapsody.

During a 1970s dance sequence our catsuit-clad group of 10 'The Reverbs' are positioned in five pairs on each point of a star-shaped troupe. One of the pair wears a 'backpack' with a number of glittery human-shaped cut outs strung together, descending from life-sized to smaller and smaller figures. The partner, positioned behind, uses a pole to hook the first, drawing out the people paper-chain effect, therefore creating the 3D illusion as per the video. Got it? Good.

Oh Danny boy

In only our second day of involvement, us late arrivals find ourselves in the first rehearsal to take place in the London Olympic stadium, therefore avoiding the rather less glamorous car park in Dagenham where the majority of the cast have been based until then.

Lighting technicians and sound guys are beetling away in the rafters while down below, us 5,000 volunteers are guided around the arena and walked through our positions. Towards the end of the night it begins to rain and we're told we can leave slightly earlier than our stated 10pm finish.

My small team are the only ones on stage when suddenly the lights are switched on for the first time; shortly afterwards, music booms from the speakers, vibrating through my very being. I turn my face up to the rain and begin to dance.

Noticing an anorak-clad dancer across the other side of the stage we shimmy towards each other. "This is awesome," I yell, still jigging away. "I know," says the boogying hooded figure looking up; it's Danny Boyle.

The Oscar-winning film director who has been charged with overseeing the opening ceremony endears himself to every one of the cast and crew. Applauding all us volunteers as we leave rehearsals, appreciative of the time we've given to be shaped into some sort of cohesive performers – many of us never having attempted anything like this before – his sheer joy at the whole process, despite the mounting pressure, is infectious.

During rehearsal a hashtag is displayed on screens around the venue imploring '#keepthesecret'. And we all do, in no small part down to our loyalty to Boyle. I even keep the secret despite working at a newspaper at the time and when phoning in to a radio station to rail against the negativity swamping the Games.

Oh, what a night

The cast head to the holding camp – basically a giant marquee at the east end of the Olympic park – during the early afternoon ahead of our nighttime performance.

Squealing punks are taking photos of NHS nurses who in turn are hugging industrial revolution workers. Half-eaten packed lunches are nibbled on, coat hangers are swinging on rails from recently grabbed costumes, people loll on the grass doing each other's make-up – just bedlam – wonderful, thrilling, buzzing, anticipatory bedlam.

Our holding station is a 30-minute walk from the stadium so timing is crucial. Tannoy announcements indicate when it's each sector's time to go. Us 'reverbs' are part of the 'Thanks Tim' cast – no one had a clue who this Tim fella was until watching the show back the next day – the main dance sequence going through Britain's musical decades of the 60s, 70s, 80s, 90s and noughties.

We are almost last to go on stage before the athlete parade begins, so we set off giggling, fully costumed up in full-on Lycra catsuits with additional arm and foot 'wings', crossing over a footbridge and waving to the astonished drivers below.

On the night I look skyward from my holding position at the stadium, gobsmacked to see a man in a tuxedo and a lady in a dress dropping from the sky. Amusingly, the cast are the last people to know it's the 'Queen' leaping out of the helicopter alongside 'James Bond', making their grand entrance into the stadium. During rehearsals we'd seen the helicopter and parachutists but presumed it was a security thing.

We wait in Vom Three, a gross-sounding name for one of five long tentacles that stretch through the bowels of the building and into different entrances around the stadium. We've heard the music so many times during rehearsals we know exactly at which point we're to enter. From our holding position we see glimmers of sparkle coming from the stage, lights dancing, punks leaping, music booming. I can't wait to get out there.

We wear earpieces with transmitters but as usual, mine falls out early on, so I just scamper onto the stage without paying too much mind to, you know, hearing the instructions from the stage manager.

The seats in the stadium are close to the track, tapering into the darkness beyond, making the stadium feel almost cosy, like a front room. I'm just able to see the people in the first few rows.

I jig onto the stage, dance a little, dash off, remove my 'reverb backpack', run 200m round the track to the point where I pick up a lit flare, running further round the track while thrusting said flare in the air all the while avoiding setting my lacquered hair on fire; after putting the now dud flare in a bucket of water off stage I head back out into the throng with arms waving in the air like reeds singing, 'I'm Forever Blowing Bubbles', 'dance' up a steep ramp, dash through the 'house' on stage past internet inventor Tim Berners-Lee, out the back of the house and on to the Tor for some final dancing and then – boom, hands held aloft, the music stops and the lights blaze.

It was only then I realise, truly, how many people are in the stadium. A beat of silence and then an almighty roar erupts. Blinking rapidly, I never want the moment to end.

Night fever
We've been told to vacate the stadium and the park immediately after our performance so that we don't add to the footfall of people leaving the area. But, well, we are just about the last ones to perform and as we dash out of

the stadium all the athletes are coming in. Two of us try to blend in with the throng of fans and army personnel lining the route – in our catsuits – and proceed to cheer every single athlete into the stadium.

"Tom Daley, Tom – do you like my catsuit? I've just been in the opening ceremony."

"Good luck Usain!"

Athletes are swapping pin badges with each other, fans and the military – it's wonderful.

After the last athletes have gone we traipse back towards the holding station. We're scooped up by security guards in a buggy telling us we have to move quickly as the fireworks will be going off all around the park shortly. Loafing about in a firework zone in flammable material is presumably unwise.

So we're dropped near the changing area where half a dozen of us sit on a small grassy hill and watch the fireworks bookend the night, me, the only one still in my costume.

Part of this article was first published in 'How it feels to… dance at the Olympics' in The Sunday Times Magazine on 17 July 2016.

2

THAT TIME I FELT WONDERFUL
AFTER A SPECIAL MOMENT
WITH A SPECTATOR

It's so quiet you can hear the chalk dust hit the floor in London's North Greenwich arena. I'm watching a gripping drama play out alongside fellow gymnastics fans at the culmination of the men's team event at the London 2012 Olympic Games.

Moments earlier, a cacophonous cheer had erupted as Britain won its first men's team Olympic medal for 100 years. Max Whitlock, Louis Smith, Sam Oldham, Kristian Thomas and Dan Purvis have finished their routines and currently sit in second position in the men's team final. Second! An astonishing achievement considering making the final eight teams was the pre-competition target.

But now I'm transfixed, as arguably the greatest male gymnast ever, Kohei Uchimura, takes to the pommel horse. The last man to perform in the whole competition, we presume he'll go through his routine cleanly, the accompanying high score enabling Japan to leapfrog

Britain and likely finishing second behind runaway winners China, with our boys still in an incredible third place.

But, unbelievably, the man known for elegance and consistency despite crazy difficult routines, makes a mistake. Kohei uncharacteristically falls out of his dismount in an inelegant struggle, which is when the silence descends.

Moment in time

All eyes turn to the scoreboard, a stunned silence smothers the arena. Kohei's score flashes up. It's low and Japan drop out of the medals into an agonising fourth, Britain stay in second and Ukraine are now in third.

The crowd erupts, cheering the beaming GB boys who are jumping up and down, coaches slapping their backs, hugging and constantly looking back up to the big screen to make sure this is really happening.

It's happening, fellas. I'm here, and I can't believe it either. Grinning from ear to ear, tears in my eyes, I can't believe I'm here to witness a waft-me-down-with-a-leotard moment in British gymnastics' history.

I'm here on my own so peer at those around me, catching eyes with fellow Brits and spectators from other countries, smiling at everybody, which is reciprocated at every turn, all of us caught up in an I-was-there sporting moment.

Then I see the elderly Japanese ladies. Sat directly behind me, the four are statue-still, eyes glistening. My smile fades. I catch their eye and put my hand to my heart in an 'I feel for you' gesture. They smile weakly.

I turn back to the scenes in front of me a little subdued. Japan's style of gymnastics is a joy to watch and the team deserve to be medal winners. Sport can be oh so cruel.

Celebrations are ongoing for the home crowd but a murmur begins to ripple around the arena and the gymnasts have not left the building. Something's afoot.

The Japanese coaches have put in a complaint about Uchimura's score. They contend that the judges valued his dismount incorrectly. If the review is successful, Kohei's score will be improved resulting in a change in the medal places. This is big.

I turn to the ladies behind me and tell them, via hand gestures to hold on – both palms raised towards them, then moving my hand horizontally side to side, and then pointing to the scoreboard – indicating there might be a change. They look hopefully towards the screen.

Waiting in the wings
I used to be a gymnast, I've watched the burgeoning sport all my life and I'm thrilled the Brits have just made history. I'm a happy bunny whichever way this goes.

I do have a soft spot for 23-year-old Kohei, though. He's brought so much joy to gymnastics fans around the world and is a hero in his home country.

Just seven months after the devastating earthquake and tsunami that decimated Japan in March 2011, Kohei became the first male gymnast to win three consecutive all-around world titles, and he did it in Tokyo.

I was there too and sat smiling next to Japanese journalists who shoved laptops aside to watch, clap and cheer as Kohei smashed his final piece of apparatus – the high bar – providing a moment of solace in a devastating period for the country. So there's an element of sadness to his error just over one year later, and the team's current fourth place.

Ten minutes we wait. Ten long minutes as the judges huddle together and watch and re-watch the routine. Initially it adds to the excitement but then we start getting antsy, particularly the Ukrainians who are set to lose the most out of this decision.

It goes the way of Japan. Uchimura's score is improved, the Japanese win silver and Britain a still sensational bronze. The Ukrainians, though, are gutted.

They're out of the medals.

I turn to the ladies, point at them, give them a double thumbs up and a big smile. The relief and joy amongst them is palpable as they turn and celebrate with each other. One of the ladies then turns to me and says, "Oooch-e-moora-mama, Oooch-e-moora-mama", while pointing at one of the ladies.

I'm baffled. Then it dawns on me what she's saying. I turn to the now smiling Japanese lady on the left who I now know is Kohei Uchimura's mother. She bows, smiles, takes my hand and presses it to her face.

3

THAT TIME I WAS
A STUNTWOMAN IN A FILM

"You're the first actresses we've seen," say the excitable check-in staff as we hand over our flight tickets. My sister and I look behind us to see who they're talking to. Turns out they mean us.

We have been hired by a film company as 'stuntwomen' for a feature film due to our high-level gymnastics abilities. Our team, Camberley Gymnastics Club, are currently rated second in Britain.

The British team champions, Heathrow Gymnastics Club, had initially been approached to source a couple of gymnasts but concerned parents cited looming school exams and passed on the opportunity.

My club was next up, and our coaches called my family at home late one night. My mum initially had the same reservations about exams but my dad, luckily, was all over wanting us to have the opportunity.

He argued we'd be hanging around on set all day and would have plenty of time to revise for our respective upcoming A levels and GCSEs. So that's why an 18-year-old and 16-year-old Brit are boarding a flight to what was then Yugoslavia, causing unexpected excitement among the airport staff.

So the film. Initially called Bull Dance, the straight-to-video extravaganza is inexplicably renamed Forbidden Sun years later. The story follows Paula, a newbie American gymnast, played by actress Samantha Mathis, arriving on a 'Greek' island to train and study with fellow Olympians.

One of the other gymnasts is assaulted and descends into a crazed spiral involving local mythology, and, not to spoil it or anything, ends up doing a death dance with a bull. Sadly it missed out on Oscar nominations that year.

Lights, camera, action

On arriving in the coastal town of Split, we settle into the hotel, a taxi arriving shortly afterwards to drop us at a beautiful, sunny, market-laden town square.

We enter an old run-down historic building and descend into a dark, dank, damp basement. Inside we come across an altogether different scene.

An oldie-worldy building, atmospheric in its drip, drip, drip of leaks, houses cameras, lights, actors, technicians, and, the focus of it all, the gym set.

It's another world.

We are introduced to the actors including one Robert Beltran, notable now for his role as Commander Chakotay in Star Trek: Voyager. I'll be doubling for Mathis who somehow manages to go on and star in Broken Arrow with Christian Slater, despite being in this film.

We look super similar with blonde straight hair and are the same height, so we're a good fit. We'd not been asked what we looked like when initially telephoned by the film company so this was luck rather than judgement on anyone's part. I'm fitted out in an identical all-in-one pale pink outfit to Mathis, sans underwear as knicker lines show up in filming, apparently. The costume ladies ask me to make sure it fits okay so I promptly up-end myself and walk about on my hands around the costume area.

Seeing the film for the first time is a joy. The camera starts filming me from behind, starting at my ankles for the run up to the vault and as I run forward my big pink Lycra-clad bottom slowly fills the screen. Marvellous. I'm just pleased the premiere was ditched for the small screen.

Safety first

We are supposed to be Olympic gymnasts in the film but cruddy apparatus means we keep the routines simple, stupidly simple. Like young kids could do what we are doing. But with most things gymnasticky, you can do something easy and people are impressed. This very much works in our favour in this instance.

We are told by director Zelda Barron to make up the routines as we see fit, as long as they start and end in a specified way, enabling a seamless continuity link with the actors during the editing process.

My older sister, Caroline, meanwhile, is doubling for one Renee Estevez, sister of actors Emilio Estevez and Charlie Sheen and daughter of The West Wing 'president', actor Martin Sheen.

Except for Caroline donning a long brown wig, their colouring and body types are similar enough to be a good fit. Not so much the blonde, wavy-haired actress Viveka Davis for whom Caroline also doubles to shoot the final dramatic stunt in the movie.

This involves a handspring over a heavily sedated bull. There's no mention of health and safety – this is filmmaking 1980s style. Luckily the idea is ditched when the aforementioned heavily sedated bull won't move to the place they want to film the sequence, so a rubbish pretend bull is used instead. Rubbish for the film but probably best for the health of my sister.

Meanwhile, I'm lolling about at the hotel one night having been at the set all day when the phone rings. Can I please go back to the set immediately? One of the Yugoslavian gymnasts has ripped a big old blister on her hand and can't do a bar routine. Can I do it instead?

Okey doke, think I. Into a taxi I get and soon I'm at the set. Turns out I am doing the stunt for actress Renee Props... and I look nothing like her. I'm quite excited it's her though because she's apparently dating Chad Lowe, brother of my 80s crush, Rob. Heady days indeed.

Saving the day

Height wise we match up but that's where the similarities end. Renee has short dark hair, tanned skin and nail-polished fingers. My straight blonde hair, fair skin and no make-up look couldn't be more opposite.

Before I know it I'm ushered into a coach-cum-dressing-room – literally as glamorous as it sounds – being told that if we don't get this scene done tonight the film cannot go on as it is massively over time and budget.

So I'm standing in the middle of the bus surrounded by costumes, mirrors, make-up and what feels like every single person mentioned in the closing credits of a movie. Local people peer through the windows at intervals while I'm in various states of undress.

One person is slathering me in fake tan, another painting my nails, another attaching a short dark wig to my head... using Sellotape. My eyes still water remembering the pain taking it off afterwards. Finally ready to go, I'm led to the basement, told to make up a routine and let's go.

I start strapping on my handguards but I'm quickly asked what I'm doing. Wearing handguards, I say. But the actress didn't wear handguards in the continuity clip, I'm told. Okay, say I, but I can't do bars unless I wear handguards. A brief impasse was resolved as time was of the essence. I wear the handguards.

I'm a one-take wonder, completing a basic routine, and dismounting in the suggested way. The movie is saved! Probably.

My sister loves the whole experience, going on to train as an actress in New York. Me? It's fine when we're actually doing stuff but waiting around on set for hours and hours doing nothing is bor-ing. My dad was right, there was plenty of time to revise for my exams, and no teenager likes that.

4

THAT TIME SPORT
SAVED MY SOUL

"These past few months have not been easy," my horoscope tells me. "Perhaps you came up against an unwanted turn in your career, money anxieties, a change in where you live, or in a love relationship."

My head sinks to the desk and rests on the pillowiness of my arms, absorbing the fact that not only do all four currently apply to me but I'm so desperate I'm reading horoscopes. The unwanted turn in my career? The recent collapse of my seven-year-old business, I presume.

Money anxieties? Tame for the fact that the business disintegrates owing tens of thousands of pounds. Fortuitously, my business-partner-cum-boyfriend and I had acted on early advice to set up the business as a limited company, leaving comparatively little personal liability. Still, a loan here, a personal borrowing there and I'm still a good few thousand pounds in debt.

What else? Oh yes. 'There will be a change in a love relationship.' Breaking up with my boyfriend and said business partner of nigh on ten years. No one advised me what precautions to take in that instance – perhaps I could have set it up as a limited relationship to negate that damage?

Next? There may be 'a change in where you live'. I'd moved back in with my parents. Not ideal, nevertheless their concern is appreciated, their hugs invaluable and their hesitant advice, touching.

I'm broken, disorientated, houseless, manless, businessless and jobless but there's only one direction I can head from this shambles and that's up. There's only one thing for it. That's right, make a list.

Crushed

When I'm at my lowest ebb I sit down and write a list of 100 things I want to do. Not necessarily that year, just at some point.

Along with some traditional ideas such as travelling round Australia in a campervan and skiing in Canada, the list includes some loopy, difficult to achieve ideas. Setting off a controlled avalanche is one, although I suspect I'm thinking Roadrunner-like plunger rather than the more likely pressing 'return' on a keyboard these days.

Another oddity? Being able to crack an egg using one hand. I tick this off the list but I'm not sure cracking the egg and letting the innards dribble through my fingers into a bowl is quite what I mean.

It's inevitable that sport features heavily, it's the constant thread that runs throughout my life. One sport item on my list is to attend a major football tournament. Handily, Euro 2004 in Portugal is coming up in a few months so I set my sights on that.

My ex had bought me out of the flat we owned, I'd paid personal debts and so I had money, time and no ties. And no excuses.

I was at my least confident so I just took it one step at a time. First, get tickets.

On the day the tickets become available via an England Fans phone line (you think getting tickets via the internet is bad) I'm on a temp job.

I ask to take my lunch break at 9am so that I can start calling the ticket line as soon as it opens. Back from my 'lunch break' at 10am it takes me until 3pm of constant redialling to get through – I'm not entirely sure the company got their money's worth out of me that day.

When I finally hear a voice I'm so excited I breezily ask for two tickets to England versus France and two tickets for England versus Croatia, both matches to be played in Lisbon.

I'm asked for two England fan membership numbers to buy the tickets. I only have my number and I don't want to miss out just because I have no one to go with so I buy one ticket for each match. I'm in.

Two weeks before the first England match I start to look at accommodation and flights. Having lived in Albufeira during a university placement I feel comfortable staying in the coastal tourist town in the Algarve, so this is where I book my fortnight's accommodation.

The matches are being played in Lisbon, a three-hour coach ride away, but I'll happily spend days on the beach before watching two games of football every evening when I don't have match tickets.

Match made in heaven

England's first game is against France in the group stage. I head to Lisbon on the coach, soak up the atmosphere in the Square next to the Estádio da Luz, then make my way to my seat two hours before kick off.

This is a big moment for me. I recognise it has taken a lot of courage when I was feeling so low to realise this particular dream. My dad told me afterwards that I looked so pale when he dropped me off at the train station on my way to the airport. But the thing about this whole thing is this: I was more fearful of missing the opportunity than fearful of taking it. What's that Mark Twain phrase? 'Twenty years from now, you will be more disappointed by the things that you didn't do than by the ones you did.' I spent much of that low time sourcing motivational quotes, too.

On entering the stadium I deliberately look at the floor until I find my seat, I put my bag down, take a deep breath and turn around.

The stadium is stunning. Lush green manicured-to-within-an-inch-of-its-life grass and the growing anticipation of a cracking match in a few hours time made my emotions bubble to the surface. I'm happy for the first time in a long while.

I call my dad and he can hear it in my voice. The real me still exists in the shell of me. I had the best conversation I've ever had with my dad that day.

In good company
After I hang up, I sit quietly, absorbing the growing excitement, watching more and more fans pile into the stadium. Then, I freeze.

My neighbour has arrived and appears to be 20-stones worth of beer and pies wrapped in skin. A bristled head sits atop a melee of tattoos and his flabby torso spills into my seat, encroaching on my personal space, which is fine, not a problem mate.

I'm a solitary 5ft 2ins female football fan so the sight of the exact stereotype of an English hooligan is unwelcome. Nevertheless, you don't guarantee a Des Lynam-alike neighbour so I grin nervously at him as we await kick-off.

Throughout the game, a thriller in which England end up on the wrong end of a 2-1 result, beer is swilled and a relentless barrage of football chants emanate from my neighbour's fleshy lips. By the end of the match I am sharing his beer, hugging his bear-like frame and duetting with him to the stadium's tunes. My prejudice, it seems, is unwarranted.

After negotiating a tricky group also including Switzerland and Croatia, England are set to play hosts Portugal in the quarter finals. I am due to fly home the day before the match, however, as I don't have a ticket.

That night it's my birthday, so I head to a bar and watch Germany get knocked out of the tournament in the group stages by the Czech Republic. I meet a couple of Norwegian girls wearing Portugal and Italy football shirts (Norway have surprisingly not made it to the finals). They ask if I'm going to the game in a couple of days. Sadly not, I tell them, I don't have a ticket. "Do you want one?" is their response. "Hell yeah," is mine.

So they go outside the bar to call someone in Lisbon and next thing I know they're knocking on the window to attract my attention. "It's £250. Do you want it?"

I pause for a split second before breaking into a big grin. "Yeah she wants it," they confirm to the anonymous ticket-genie. The next day I miss my flight and instead ready myself for the crunch match the following day.

Ticket genie

I'm given instructions to meet 'Bob' outside a hotel in Lisbon the next day, four hours before the match kicks off. I join the Norwegian girls on the bus to Lisbon and then venture off to find 'Bob'.

Venture being the appropriate word as I weave my way around the back streets that make up Portugal's capital city. Eventually finding the nominated hotel I await nervously for my golden ticket. A suave looking guy in a business suit appears from the bowels of the hotel, looks at me and gives me an envelope with the name 'Desmond' on it.

"Have you counted the money?" he asks me.

"Well, yes," I say, confused.

This, combined with the whole 'Desmond' thing makes me think I've got the wrong person, but with a ticket to the match in hand I'm not going to quibble over niceties.

With no guarantee this is a kosher ticket I nervously queue very early on to get into the ground. Amazingly, it works and in I go and the first person I see is former England manager Terry Venables.

"Terry, Terry I'm here on my own. Can I get a picture with you?"

"You're here on your own? Come here you nutter," says El Tel affectionately as he gives me a warm hug.

Game time

I take my seat in the stadium amongst a melee of England and Portugal fans, usually a no, no at football matches but which, for this tournament, makes for a special atmosphere.

To my right sits a Norwegian fan who has never missed an England international and to my left, a couple of Burberry-wearing England fans continuously chant intermittently with the Portuguese supporters. "Por-too-gaal," "En-ger-land," "Por-too-gall," "En-ger-land," reverberates around the stadium stuffed with excitable football fans.

As usual, England go out dramatically after Wayne Rooney limps off early in the second half with a broken foot, England have a perfectly good goal disallowed (yawn) and then, for the fourth time in four penalty shoot-outs, we go out with el capitan David Beckham missing the vital first penalty. The Portuguese fans around me sympathise.

"It was a good game."

"You were unlucky."

I grin mournfully until after about the 21st offer of commiseration I get a bit tetchy and make my way out of the ground.

I arrange to meet with my Norwegian pals so that we can make our way to the station together to catch the late-night bus back to the coast.

Rather joyfully the Portuguese authorities decide to close the tube station that will take us back to the city and our bus. No other transport is heading to the city and taxis are about as scarce as an England fan smiling.

Us three girls decide to walk to the next tube station and on the way flag down a car to ask two lads and their grandfather the whereabouts of the nearest tube stop. Miles away apparently so they offer to give us a lift into the city.

So this is how I find myself stuffed in the back of the smallest car in the world with two Norwegian girls on my right, a smiling Portuguese grandfather on my left ("Hey boys can you take a photo of me and the girls in the back... but don't show the wife!") and two ecstatic football fans driving us slowly through the pulsating streets of Lisbon.

People are dancing on cars like scenes from the TV show Fame, passengers leap out of cars, dance a jig and dive back through the car window, legs akimbo.

Flags are lunatically waving in the balmy night and an English girl, trapped in a celebration of her team's demise, is smiling quietly to herself, knowing that despite the night's result, she's on the way to getting her mojo back.

Caveat: I'm aware of my opposing takes on ticket touts within different stories in this book. What can I say? A sports fan's gotta do what a sports fan's gotta do.

5

THAT TIME AN INTERNATIONAL
SPORTING EVENT WAS INCIDENTAL
TO US SPECTATORS

A trip to Australia isn't complete without partaking in a
major sporting event – well for me anyway. So when I
bump into a couple at the Kirribilli Wharf and they tell me
they're off to the Sydney Cricket Ground to watch
Australia versus New Zealand in a One Day International,
I soon find my own walk abandoned.

A quick visit to a ticketing website and shortly
thereafter I'm on a bus from Elizabeth Street headed to
Moore Park. I am surrounded by bare-chested men
wearing Santa hats so I figure this is the right bus.

Finding it nigh on impossible to find my seat at the
stadium, made more difficult by seeking help from the
stewards, I plonk myself in a single seat at the end of a row
and hope for the best.

My match-watching companions to my right are an
amorous couple who chomp their way through ice-creams,
sandwiches and a number of beers. Presumably they've

taken out a small loan to pay for the insanely expensive stadium food. Directly in front of me are two multi-coloured afros with people attached. When a four is hit the 'fros rise, an arm extends from each, ebbing and flowing from left to right in perfect unison.

To my left, six lads are dressed in flags and blue-felt cloth caps while fluorescent sun cream is smeared warrior-like across their faces. All relatively harmless considering I could have been sat next to the full-figured fella I passed on the way in wearing a canary yellow catsuit.

Further down the stand I see a bunch of New Zealand fans inexplicably wearing surgeons operating gowns, hat included; all very amusing when en masse yet it's heads down and ignoring their outfit when off to the toilet on their own.

The breathless sighs of a bagpipe indicate I am sat in front of the match's unofficial entertainment. Luckily the guy is pretty good as he starts up the first of many renditions of 'I'm an Australian', which sounds distinctly odd wheezing out of bagpipes.

The more beer sodden people become, the more they join in, so when, towards the end of the match the pipe player strikes up 'Jingle Bells', a cacophony of inebriated cricket fans belt out the well known Christmas song. Mildly amusing is the pie-eating beer guzzler who is tapping his foot and slapping his considerable thigh in time to the music.

Drone on
A middle-aged Irish guy in front of me, in all innocence, tells the inebriated local next to him that this is his first ever cricket match. The Aussie then proceeds to explain cricket from its early century beginnings through to today's players... for the next four hours, without pausing for breath. After a while it becomes a soothing accompaniment to the match as I fade in and out of the interesting bits.

Kiwi outfielder, Millsy, gets involved in a bit of beach ball action when he volleys an inflatable ball back into the crowd. That is, until an overzealous steward nabs it, stabs it, and deflates it to not so affectionate calls from the crowd.

Later, the crowd rises as one and I wonder if I've missed a catch. Not so, they are trying to see if another inflatable ball – this one four times the size of the previous one – is going to end up on the pitch. A chorus of cheers erupts if the front row spectators can keep the ball in play.

Settling in after lunch, a kerfuffle erupts at the opposite end of the ground. A five-metre long beer-cup snake soon arises on a sea of hands. Twenty minutes later and not to be outdone, my side produce a similar length snake, which is beaten a short while later by our opposite numbers. Resigned applause from my lot rings out – we know when we're beaten.

Finally, an energetic Mexican wave starts up, culminating in plastic bottles, ticker tape and the aforementioned beer cups hurled up on the crest of a wave then raining down like sea spray rippling round the ground. Oh, and the world's best cricketers are slugging it out on the pitch against their arch rivals, relegated to just a sideshow.

6

THAT TIME I CAMPED OVERNIGHT FOR WIMBLEDON TICKETS

Since when does Wimbledon have hot days? The day you're at the tournament having had no sleep after camping overnight for tickets in a nearby field, that's when.

Camping out for day-sale tickets is like sleeping overnight, in the old days, for the launch of a new Apple product, but the sport version. A limited number of tickets are released on the day of the quintessentially English tennis tournament, including premium tickets for Centre Court and No 1 court matches.

Certainly if there's a big match, such as your Murralds or your Feds, you're going to have to dig out your musty camping gear for its annual outing to sleep overnight in a queue to even be in with a chance of nabbing a ticket.

But don't for one minute think once you arrive in the field next to the lauded grounds that this will be a haphazardous free-for-all. Good grief no. This is Wimbledon, publishers of a glossy booklet entitled, 'A

Guide To Queueing'. You'll notice I said booklet not leaflet. This thing is 28-pages long – 28 pages – and includes a section headlined 'The Queue Code Of Conduct'. My favourite, favourite bit states, 'Queue jumping is not acceptable and will not be tolerated'. Quite right. I'm surprised this is number four on the list – I think it should be top – nevertheless, I'm sated by the fact it is the only capitalised item out of the nine codes.

Quiet, please

So my Kiwi mate Kathy and I arrive at said field one Friday night after work having hoiked camping kit from our office. We're surprised to see the field already half full. We're shown to the end of the line by a steward and then literally we pitch a tent in our place in the queue. Genius. This is a huge relief to us Brits who seethe silently at queue dodgers, willing said person to feel our vibes of fury masked by a polite demeanour.

We're hoping we're early enough in the queue to get Centre Court tickets to see Andy Murray play 30th seed Victor Troicki in a third round match. After a quick tent count, however, we realise we're unlikely to be high enough up the queue for these tickets. Ultimately it depends what the people in front of us choose come the morning, but we should be clear for No 1 court tickets.

Meanwhile, we wrestle with our tent, a broken pole not conducive to a quick process. Our fellow queue dwellers loll about watching, beer in hand, presumably having gone through the same initiation shortly before. We follow suit once we're set, watching newbies struggle while tucking into Pimms-in-a-can.

As night falls, an official goes tent to tent asking noisy types to be quiet as a courtesy to other campers. At 10pm. Ah Wimbledon, you're so civilised.

Kathy and I are pooped and stuffed full of cold chips and ketchup, one of a minimal choice of foods available from huts dotting the field's edges.

We're ready to sleep, but of course we don't. You just don't. So the 6am alarm call from the stewards, asking us to please start getting up and pack away our tents, is unwelcome.

Queue gardens

At 7.30am we're given a wrist band to wear to indicate we're high enough in the queue to buy No 1 court tickets – Centre Court have indeed all gone – when eventually arriving at the ticket office.

The hallowed gates don't open until 10.30am and with the first match not starting on the main courts until noon we realise this is going to be a long day.

Until then, it's a case of shuffling forwards from time to time, tent kit an' all. You can actually leave the queue to head to the Portakabin loos, something I manage to avoid.

Once we make it to the edge of the field, The Queue, (that's right, it's capitalised) snakes onto the pavement and along the road towards the Wimbledon entrance. Us overnighters are either splayed out horizontally on roll mats trying to have a cat nap or sat chatting on the pavement with fellow queuers.

I tell a story about the time I'd been at Wimbledon as a teen. While walking around the courts a guy came up to me and asked for my autograph. I looked at him and said, "What me?"

"Yes," he said.

"Me?"

"Yes."

"Okay then," and promptly signed his programme.

Game, set and match

Finally and joyfully we make it inside to the Wimbledon turf, the night's discomfort and the morning's sleepiness ebbing away. Before we can relax, though, there's more queueing to do. It's off to lost luggage to stash our tents. We hear about a family who had set off at 4am to get to the event early, yet were too late and had to head straight home. We're grateful to be in.

Once we dispose of said tent we're free to enjoy the day. We head to the outside courts to watch some actual tennis before heading to our coveted No 1 court seats.

We watch one of the headline matches of the day as the Czech Republic's Tomas Berdych beats Russia's Nikolay Davydenko; Germany's Tommy Haas is victorious in a five-set thriller against Croatia's Marin Cilic, completed from the previous day; and Germany's Sabine Lisicki easily beats Russia's Svetlana Kuznetsova.

We can hear the roar from the crowd on Centre Court as Murray beats Troicki in three straight sets, and we're not in any way secretly pleased that we haven't missed a thriller. We melt sleepily into our seats, the repetitious thwack, thwack, thwack followed by a smattering of applause lulling us into a doze, eyes drooping in the mid-afternoon sun.

7

THAT TIME I ESCAPED OVER A FENCE FROM A SPORTS AWARDS PARTY

As I read the email, my relief is short-lived and quickly turns to mortification. It's probably best if I start 24 hours earlier.

I'd been invited to a glamorous end-of-year sports awards so I glam up and head to a TV studio in west London for the annual event.

Towards night's end I'm acutely aware I need to get the last train home. Chatting with a couple of other attendees, I find out one is in the same position and the other is driving and happy to drop us at the station.

So we leave the building and somehow take a wrong turn, ending up surrounded by a maze of fences and security gates. I head towards one turnstile-type exit, saying, "I'm pretty sure I came in this way".

The other two are unsure and reluctant to try said gate so yours truly tentatively pushes the revolving mechanism and heads through.

It's a tight squeeze but I make it. I register quickly, though, that there's no way back and realise I am in even more of a pickle, surrounded on all sides by more fencing with no obvious way out.

I turn to the dynamic duo to whom I am now separated suggesting that perhaps this isn't right after all. Time is ticking, we need to get to the train station, so I suggest they head back the way we came while I find my way out of my current predicament.

If they go and get the car I'll meet them on the exit road ready to head to the station. If it's getting late, they should just head off and I'll make my own way.

Jo-proof fence

Off they go. I turn back to my quandary. What to do. Only one thing I can do, keep going. So I follow the line of the fence away from the bright lights of the building. I can see where I need to be I just can't get there.

Tottering along in my fancy shoes and sparkly knee-length frock I'm beginning to feel like a fancily-dressed animal in a zoo, prowling the perimeter fence. I just need to get beyond the barrier and I'm free.

Time is ticking, I need to get the train and two other people are waiting for me. Moving towards a dark patch away from the lights, I make a decision.

Removing my shoes I hurl one, then the other over the fence to freedom. My handbag follows shortly afterwards. In stockinged feet, I begin to scale the fence. Yep. The wire dents the soft flesh on my soles and palms but I'm making steady progress up the nigh-on eight-foot high barrier.

On reaching the top I hoik my legs over commando stylee, go down a few more rungs on the other side then leap cat-like onto the grass beyond. I'm free!

The option to find somewhere dark to escape isn't conducive to finding said shoes and bag so I scrabble about on my hands and knees feeling around in the dark, finding first one shoe, then the other. Shortly afterwards I come across my bag. Perfect. I can now find my buddies and hopefully make it in time for the last train. I reach into my bag for my phone to check the time.

I'd forgotten to close the zip. My phone's missing.

Oh joy.

Crouching down I frantically feel around the grass for the second time.

Tick tock

I now have no idea what the time is but I do know that if I don't get that train I'll have a super expensive taxi ride back to my house the other side of London. I can't even call mates nearby to see if I can stay over. This is fun.

Abandoning the search for my phone I run towards the station, which, to be fair, is only half a mile away. I make it with minutes to spare and breathlessly update my amused fellow attendee who's waiting on the platform.

The next morning I receive an email from security at the studios: "Can you call us please? We think we have your phone."

Relief floods through me but then I blanch. Either someone just happened to come across my phone in the grass in a random part of the complex or... or... I pale. CCTV.

8

THAT TIME I REALISED MY BOYFRIEND TOTALLY UNDERSTOOD MY LOVE OF SPORT

Having been turned down for a London 2012 Olympics volunteer role, auditioned twice to be in the opening ceremony yet ended up a reserve, and got nothing from applying for £2,500 worth of tickets in the ballots, I'm gutted.

Rewind seven years and I'm on the verge of moving to Sydney from the UK, until one rainy summer's day, London snatches the vote to host the Games from hot favourites, Paris.

There's no way I can move to Sydney now the Olympic Games are going to be in my back yard, so I put the move on hold, and promptly move to east London. I even aim to clear the decks of my freelance work for the whole 17-day period.

I now lived three miles from the Olympic stadium and had hunkered down waiting for any opportunity to get involved. Opportunities that had now come to nothing.

Some friends of my boyfriend, Jason, kindly offer us two of their four tickets for a morning session of athletics, so I'm now at least going but sport is my lifeblood, I'm still so disappointed not to be more involved.

Element of surprise

"Some friends of mine are in London," says Jason one weeknight in April, three months before the start of the Games." We're going for dinner with them on Wednesday."

My first thought on seeing my older sister, Caroline, who lives on the south coast in Brighton, and my parents – Hampshire – as we walk in the restaurant is 'how bizarre they just happen to be in the same restaurant as us on this night'. I know.

After realising something is afoot I'm further surprised when seated at a long table with an additional four empty seats. Just room enough for my younger sister, Ali, husband Charlie and my eight- and five-year-old nieces, Lucy and Milly, who arrive shortly after.

All I'm told is that this is an early surprise for a big birthday of mine looming in June. At the end of a meal filled with surreptitious glances and smiles, Jason hands Lucy eight gold envelopes.

On opening the first, Lucy pulls out a card inside and reads, "Ali, Caroline, Charlie, Garth, Jacky, Jason, Lucy and Milly invite you to attend the Archery at Lord's Cricket Ground on Tuesday 31 July 2012 at the London 2012 Olympics."

I promptly burst out crying. Confused by my happy tears, Milly hugs my arm and says: "If you don't win a medal, I'll make you one." Seven envelopes later and I'm off to handball, fencing, hockey, swimming, diving, all sorts… I'm stunned.

Turns out, Jason has spent hours trawling websites to find tickets, contacting friends in other countries and even setting up a spreadsheet to make sure not to buy any tickets that clash with my favourite events. My family contribute to the not insignificant cost.

Having watched me tear up at the merest hint of sporting achievement, whether it's a Brit or, well anyone really, it turns out Jason completely understands my yearning to be involved in London 2012, and my crushing disappointment at, so far, being foiled at every turn.

As a kid I used to see my dad sitting alone watching sport on TV so I would go and sit with him to keep him company. As a result, I now have a love for all things sport from football to Formula One to athletics, tennis, and, er, well snooker and darts, although the last two are my own doing.

I was also an elite gymnast until I was 17-years-old when a stress fracture in my lower back, followed by a spinal fusion operation, signalled the end of my much-loved gymnastics life.

I felt then that gymnastics was my whole raison d'être and struggled with my identity. One of the senior girls at my gym club, Karen Kennedy, ended up going to the Seoul Olympics, so not having reached my peak was hard to swallow. However, an empathy and love of all sport was sown deep into my being, which is why I was so desperate to be part of the biggest sporting drama of them all.

And there's more

Next thing I know, Jason is whispering in Lucy's ear. Unsure, she double-checks what he's asked her to say, then announces: "There's been an almighty cock-up," to giggles around the table, although maybe not her parents. "We've found some more envelopes."

A VIP ticket for the women's individual gymnastics final and two mornings at the athletics are the pièce de résistance of an unforgettable evening.

Later, I also manage to get my grubby paws on tickets for the men's 100m final, what turns out to be athletics' Super Saturday, Tom Daley in the diving and a plethora of

Paralympic tickets. But it's as I take my seat at Lord's for the archery or watch the gymnastics glass of wine in hand from a VIP vantage point that the emotions bubble over. The lengths my boyfriend and family have gone to in order to help me reach an alternative Olympic dream is now what brings me to tears.

9

THAT TIME I HAD AN INCIDENT WITH A BOY BAND WHEN I VOLUNTEERED AT A CHARITY RUN

Having given up time and effort to help at the BBC Sport Relief Mile, I wasn't expecting to get shouted at for my troubles. Then again, it's entirely my own fault. Turns out, I'm blithely unaware of the safety concerns involved when a combustible combination of boy band and screaming girls, plus mums to be fair, collide.

I've volunteered as an on-course marshal at the biennial event that sees the general public get sponsored to run either one, three or six miles. Courses are set up all over the country but I'm in the rather glamorous locale of St James's Park in London.

"Who would like to use the megaphone?" asks an event leader early that Saturday morning. My hand darts up and shortly afterwards I'm megaphoned up. My role for the day is to stay at the finish line, advising just-finished runners to keep the area clear. For hours I happily yell, "Well done guys, but can you please move through the area? Keep moving through the area, thank you." It all goes wrong when I begin to be approached by sparkly-clad girls.

"What time are JLS running?" asks the first innocent-looking girl. I had no idea they were, I tell her, but this is the end of the race so presumably they'll come through here at some point. Try hanging around here. A short time later a second, bespectacled girl approaches and I tell her the same thing. Wanting to be helpful I find out roughly what time the boys are expected to arrive and seek out both girls to tell them what I know. Glowing with helpfulness, I get back to my megaphone.

A short while later us volunteers are told by the head-volunteer types not to mention that JLS are on the way. An obsolete point at this stage as the hum of excitable fans is increasing in volume, with more and more fans inexplicably congregating near the finish area... ahem. It takes my best demanding-yet-pacifying voice to get this mass of sparkliness clear of the area, but I manage.

Until the boys arrive.

And all hell breaks loose.

Boy band on the run

The boys dash from a nearby building, barely making it to the course through the screaming throng tearing at them. A mass of people surge past me, and so, caught up in the moment, I announce, "JLS are in the house".

And that is when I'm yelled at.

"No. Bad," says the head-volunteer type as she sweeps past, the safety of the heaving swarm paramount in her mind. So bad, it turns out, that even after she's gone past me she feels the need to turn around, glare at me and repeat, "Bad", for added emphasis.

But the boys were right there, I tell myself. They weren't 'on their way' they were right frigging there. I sheepishly return to telling people to keep the area clear, my cheeks burning.

And so the noisy ball of humans makes its way round the course, JLS in front and the now hoarse young girls sprinting in their inappropriate flimsy shoes to keep up. I tell you what though, it's definitely one way to get young girls active.

10

THAT TIME I WENT EYEBALL TO
EYEBALL WITH TICKET TOUTS

I'm up at 6.45am and out the door by 7.30am but I'm not off to work, I'm on the first stage of a mission to get re-sale tickets for the sold out Andy Roddick versus Lleyton Hewitt semi-final showdown at the 2005 Australian Open taking place at Melbourne Park later that day.

Surprisingly, despite being at the ticket office by 8.30am, I'm second in line behind a Japanese lady. An hour later, a mother and her two personable teenage kids join us along with a purple velour tracksuit-wearing lady.

The mother already has tickets for herself and her husband but the kids want to come too, considering Hewitt is an Aussie, an' all. Conversation spills from both parties while I listen in, already having taken to sprawling on the concrete floor in my queuing position.

It's already toasty warm and as much as I think I'm going to be in the queue for two hours tops, it's been an early start and I need to look ahead. The last two men's matches have gone through to midnight – in their infinite wisdom, the tennis powers-that-be had introduced 7.30pm start times for some matches – so I'm aware I need to conserve my energy. I've even got a couple of bananas and two litres of water in my bag.

A short while later we are advised by stadium security that this ticket office won't be open until 12 noon and we'd be better off trying to get tickets in Federation Square, which is open now.

Swing into action

As I disappear in a haze of dust, a father and son I've met in the queue try to engage me in some chit chat. Realising I can't outrun them unless I break into a rather unsportsmanlike trot, I turn friendly compadre as we make our way to the ticket office.

There's no queue here, just a girl from Tasmania also looking for tickets. We're soon told this office won't be open until 11.30am and we should head to the Exhibition Street office, which, we're assured, is definitely open now.

Having heard this before we opted to form splinter groups. Father and son (Pat and Matt) go to Exhibition Street while Tasmania and I stay put. Pat gives me his number and tells me to call him in 15 minutes and he'll let me know if the office is open. Would Pat give me the correct number despite the fight for tickets? Apparently so.

Yes, he's tells me, the Exhibition Street office is open and a lady there is "looking after them". Tasmania and I opt to head there.

On arrival, a lady behind the counter is scouring a website for re-sale tickets. She suggests the first tickets released are more likely to be at the stadium-side box office, so, frustratingly, Tasmania and I head back to the queue where it all began. We leave Pat and Matt watching a computer screen refresh every few minutes.

By this time it is noon and a queue of around 25 people has now developed back at my starting point at the Stadium's ticket office. Swallowing my disappointment I sit down, but not before noticing Japan returned a lot earlier and is number five in the queue.

The ticket booth finally opens and clarifies what we all know – there are no tickets. A few lightweights disappear leaving Tasmania and me about 10 from the front. Tasmania goes off to get some food while I keep our place in the queue, lying flat on my back, hat perched on nose ready for a kip. Next minute, "Excuse me? Hello? Excuse me?"

Five minutes couldn't have passed yet us queuers have been asked to move to the side of the ticket office. The nice man behind me didn't want to queue jump and so woke me up. I chuckle with him but cold-shoulder the others who stepped over me to advance up the line.

Tasmania heads to the stadium when it opens at 2pm, as there are more ticket booths inside, while I stay put. Both our mobiles are running low on juice but we promise to let each other know if we have any luck.

I also keep trying a ticketing phone line but have no luck there either. Later on, tickets are released for the women's final the next day, which I relay to the other queue dwellers. A Japanese man uses my phone to try to get these tickets (I thought it might stand me in good stead with the god of tickets) but I opt to wait for tickets for local boy Hewitt.

Deuce

The flies and I enjoy reading a book for the next hour where at times I sit cross-legged, lay flat on my back, sprawl on my front, curl on my side, until a couple in the queue ahead of me ask, "Have you seen what's going on at the front?"

I stand up.

"Apparently a couple of guys have bought tickets," the couple say, "but we think they're selling them on. They're always on the phone and they keep disappearing round the back of the ticket office."

Touts.

Blood boiling and with no proof whatsoever I decide to take action. Nobody gets between me and my sport. I ask a steward if I can have a private word. We move to the side and I explain what I've just been told.

I have no proof about the people in front being touts, I say, but I am a sports journalist, I'm not working and I'm standing in the queue like everyone else and not using a press pass – I don't mind doing that – but I just want it to be fair and to alert someone to what is going on. If someone's bought a ticket, they move on and we all move forward. That's the rules. I'm English – I know how to queue properly.

The steward says she'll speak to her boss. Walking past the 'touts' on my way back to the queue one of them looks directly at me. I look straight back – eyes blazing.

Advantage me

Back in the queue I've caused a ripple of excitement after revealing I'm a journalist and then proactively going to speak to someone. For added credibility I ask the steward for her name (she gives me her security tag number) and I take my notebook out and start making 'notes'. I also sling my camera over my shoulder as if about to take pap shots.

During this excitement, my phone rings. It's Tasmania.

"Jo, I've got two tickets but they're restricted view behind the Channel 7 cameras. Is that okay?"

"Get them," I yell. "Just get me in that stadium."

I turn to my fellow queue inhabitants. "Erm. Sorry. Gotta go. I've managed to get a ticket. But I did tell the steward you guys are annoyed as well."

Shrugging their shoulders, they respond that at least it had been briefly exciting and that I looked so innocent sitting there reading my book.

So into the stadium I dash, telling security that no, my camera doesn't take video footage, a little white lie, which has its origins at the Euro 2004 football tournament in

Portugal. On entering the stadium then, security had already said I could go through when I 'helpfully' asked if they wanted to see inside the front pocket of my bag as well.

Seconds later I'm furiously throwing away four perfectly good, expensive, rechargeable batteries in case I take it upon myself to throw them at the players. The lady next to me has to bin her lipstick but caustically challenges, "So I can throw this pen at them, can I?" Apparently so.

Before long I have ticket in hand and all irritation from the heat, flies and discomfort of being in a queue for seven hours falls away. We're in. Behind a monstrous TV camera, around which we have to crane our necks to see the court, but in, nevertheless.

With our newfound good humour we call Pat to let him know how we'd managed to get tickets and to tell him to keep trying – he might get lucky, like us.

Turns out a random lady had given Pat and his son two free unwanted corporate tickets and they were currently sitting in an air-conditioned room having a cooling drink and looking forward to watching the match from the best seats in the house.

11

THAT TIME I WAS STRANDED
AT THE AIRPORT ON
A SPORTS TOUR TO SPAIN

It all starts exactly how you'd expect a sports tour to start – oddly. I don't usually approach random men at the airport to ask if they play netball but it seems my only option in this particular pickle.

I'd arrived at Alicante airport in Spain with no sign of the only other person I know on a multi-team mixed netball tour.

Ralph and I play every Tuesday night at London-based social sports club Playnetball and are supposed to have been on the same flight. I had not seen him at departures or on the plane on the way out and there's no sign of him now at the luggage carousel.

A busy time at work means I literally just booked my flight and hopped on the plane. I have no other info about where to go once I've arrived in Spain, where I'm staying or even which town the tournament is located. Ralph has all that.

I try calling Ralph while waiting for my luggage but to no avail. What to do. I know, approach a random man at the carousel. The logic behind this is that he looks like he's part of a group. Good, eh?

Stranger danger… me in this case
"Excuse me, do you play netball?"
Random man confirms that yes he plays netball, yes he's there for a netball tournament, and no he doesn't know anyone on the trip called Ralph. I thank the man and try calling Ralph again. I get through.

"I'm at the luggage carousel," say I. "Where are you?"

"At Gatwick," replies Ralph. "I thought we were on the same flight."

"Me too," say I, "Me too."

The random man I now know as Vin kindly offers me a spare seat on his team's minibus. So off I go on a 50-mile trip to Javea, hanging out with this rival squad while they settle into their villa, before heading out en masse to dinner.

A few hours later, Ralph and the rest of my actual team find me in a restaurant, having a raucous old time with two-dozen similarly inebriated people. This is the sort of thing that happens on a sports tour. At least to me.

12

THAT TIME THERE WAS NO ROOM
FOR BOYS' GYMNASTICS

"Ugh, it's a boy," comments a plaited gymnast craning her neck towards the gym club door, a ripple-effect commencing as a plethora of tiny pony-tailed heads swivel towards the little fella in question.

It's the 1980s and we're training at Surrey-based Camberley Gymnastics Club. 'Choose Life' T-shirts swamp our tiny leotard-clad bodies, Lion ointment is the crème de jour smeared on blistered hands, and we are agog at a newly installed 'foam pit' in which we can now land softly when learning new moves.

We're a decent side, consistently vying annually for title of British team champions, only once besting our arch rivals Heathrow Gymnastics Club. We even have a future Olympian in our midsts, Karen Kennedy.

Solely catering for girls, our club's facilities reflect those of gyms around the country at that time, and include two vaults, four beams, two sets of A-bars, one floor area and a tumble run. Of the six men's events only the floor area caters for both genders so this new kid would just have to make do, and only after us girls have finished our routines at that, alright? What on earth was a boy doing in our domain anyway?

Ring the changes

Our heroes are the pixie-like Russian Olga Korbut and Romania's Nadia 'perfect 10' Comaneci. Solitary male gymnast's break into our consciousness such as Valerie Liukin. The Russian competes a triple-back somersault on floor, a feat so astounding I name the family cat after him. Our other cat? Nadia, of course.

I watch women's international gymnastics competitions repeatedly, mouthing the commentator's words that become so familiar, the VHS video tapes thinning with use. I might dip into men's vault, high bar and floor but (close your ears Louis and Max) I fast-forward through pommel horse. Bo-ring. To us, men's gymnastics is just an added sideshow. The sport is all about us girls.

Back to our gym and it's not long before one of our training beams is removed to make way for a set of parallel bars, squashed in beside 'our' vault run.

A high bar surreptitiously arrives but is only erected after us girls have finished training, dismantling our precious asymmetric bars to accommodate it. We continue to be miffed. "There's just no room for boys," we grumble.

Years later and I speak to that bashful tyke who was the first boy who dared enter our gym. Nicholas Daines, now Hollywood stuntman for the likes of Harry Potter and James Bond films, and GB Masters diver to boot. It must have been intimidating for you to walk into a sporting set-up entirely geared towards girls, I say.

It was, Nicholas tells me, but I also remember that I really looked up to you girls.

Turns out there was room for us all.

13

THAT TIME I TRIED
STAND-UP COMEDY

I'm in the car park telling a Ford Fiesta one of my jokes when the first of my mates turns up to watch my looming stand-up comedy show. That's right, 'my stand-up comedy show', four words I never thought I'd say.

Three days previously I'd been a complete novice but now, following a two-and-a-half-day course, I was still a novice but now I was a novice with a show to perform.

Rewind two weeks and my boyfriend, Jason, and I are settling in for a comedy night at our local pub. As we sit waiting for the show to start, a leaflet is placed in my hand emblazoned with, 'Perform your own stand-up comedy routine!'

"There are few things more terrifying than the prospect of performing your own stand-up comedy routine in front of a paying audience of over 100 people… but this could be your chance," stated the leaflet, promoting an event to raise money for the charity Changing Faces. Jason and I look at each other. This is it. I'd recently been struggling with a lack of confidence so he'd suggested I try something out of my comfort zone. Initially, the worst thing I could think of was potholing. Not a chance. But this? This I could try.

Two weeks later and I'm preparing to go on stage alongside 10 other comedy virgins.

Getting my act together

The event is set to take place at the Abbeydale Picture House, an old run-down theatre in Sheffield, in an effort to raise money for people with facial disfigurements.

Comedian Logan Murray, tutor of the likes of Greg Davies (The Inbetweeners) and Josh Widdicombe (The Last Leg), would run the three-day course from Friday evening and over the whole weekend until the five-minute performance come Sunday evening.

Ten random souls arrive after work to a small, uninspiring conference room located down a city-centre side street for the first session. Each of us have our own reason for putting ourselves through this. One lady wants a distraction from her cancer treatment, another has left a stifling teaching career and is open to trying new experiences.

Surprisingly, most had some form of acting ability, from a former soap opera actress to a pantomime part, but I'm raw and not enjoying the early stages.

Over the next two days, Logan takes us through a series of exercises to develop our stage presence and to increase our confidence in front of an audience. Mostly I squirm during role-playing sequences and ad-libbing games but go with it as part of the whole testing myself thing.

On turning up at the run-down but atmospheric theatre on the Sunday I immediately head for the stage, leap up and stroll around to get a feel for it. However, Logan opts instead for a much, much smaller 'stage', a platform really, about one foot high, and 6ft by 4ft, positioned in front of the main stage. The idea is that the intimacy will be better with the crowd at eye level. I'm surprised at myself as I'm disappointed; I was all over wanting to be on the big stage.

Logan advises us on different ways to use the microphone – I opt to remove the microphone from the stand before moving it to one side, mainly because I think it looks more 'comediany'. I also tape a cheat sheet to the floor by my feet, with just one or two words reminding me of my next joke.

I already had a loose idea of my show prior to the course and just tweak it and add to it during the sessions. Others start that Sunday with a blank page, pretty much creating their show on the day. For some that might work but I am much happier for having some ideas I am comfortable with.

Practise what I preach

I'm a storyteller at heart so this type of delivery is my natural inclination. Logan warns story-type jokes with a big build up must deliver a big crescendo otherwise they fall flat – we've all been there – but I still choose this style.

Others opt for super-clever threads that weave through the joke, some are personal, some exceedingly frank, but what works for everyone is that all are personal and suited to the person doing the telling.

By early afternoon we start practising our sets. I start off okay but then my mind wanders or goes blank while trying to grasp the thread of my next joke. Somehow this doesn't bother me.

During the whole process I feel like I'm observing myself and wondering how I'll cope next rather than panicking. It's unlikely we'll get heckled from friends and family in the crowd, despite threats from Jason. There's nothing that can go too far wrong, apart from making a total and utter prat of yourself, obviously.

We head to the stage to practice our sets alone, with one or two watching and offering encouragement, but mostly we scatter to the wind honing scripts, muttering to ourselves and looking like the unfunniest people in the world. It's dark and cold in the theatre, which is why I opt to rehearse outside in the car park.

Ready or not, here I come

And me? I'm nervous, I guess, but I also can't wait. I'm happy with my material and now have a basic knowledge of the technical stuff – how to project to an audience, the microphone bit, making eye contact with the audience, that sort of thing.

The first five are up before the interval and I'm first on after the break, with four more following me. This works well for me as I'm able to sit and enjoy my fellow crazies' performances knowing I can review my material during the break. All get laughs – yes, we have a friendly audience of family and friends – but they get real laughs.

The interval comes and I head upstairs to the 'Green Room', a dilapidated atmospheric place, and murmur my routine to myself. It's different every time, I've never done a full run through perfectly, nevertheless, I'm ready.

After getting the audience going again with a few japes after the interval, Logan introduces me, saying I'll be backflipping down the aisle as I used to be a gymnast, and, "Heeeeere she is, Jo Gunston". I'm up.

I love it! I walk down the aisle, step onto the 'stage', remove the mike from the stand while simultaneously moving it to one side, saying, "Yeah, I don't do gymnastics anymore, bit old for that", and I'm off.

I stroll up and down the 'stage', occasionally looking down at my notes on the floor while people are laughing – actually laughing – at my jokes. I sail through.

That's not to say I'm perfect. I recognise when I've gone one ad lib too far subsequently tempering what I thought would be my best joke; I'm surprised by the joke that got the biggest laugh; I should have stuck to my gut feeling and not embellished one joke with a suggestion from Logan.

I'm confident making eye contact with the audience (except my support troupe – that would have been a step too far); I realise bang-drumming politicised jokes are not me as I try to make a joke out of a recent news item; I'm happy my jokes involving sport are a hit as that's what I know, but most of all, most of all I'm happy with myself. I've done it and I feel wonderful.

I think I'm not nervous but my hands are shaking with adrenaline when I try to put the microphone back in the stand, so I give up and just hand it to Logan as he comes on to introduce the next act.

I grin my little head off when walking back down the aisle to the applause, high-fiving one chap who holds out his palm as I stroll past. I look up and see Jason who has left his seat and is standing at the back waiting for me.

"I'm so proud of you," he says, grinning broadly. Turns out, I'm proud of me too.

ABOUT THE AUTHOR

It's hard to believe all these stories can happen to one person but not if you've met Jo Gunston. The former gymnast lives her life via the famed quote of 19th century writer Mark Twain: "Twenty years from now, you will be more disappointed by the things that you didn't do than by the ones you did."

Jo lives and breathes sport in work and in play and is publisher of lifestyle website www.sportsliberated.com. It's here you'll find more of these stories plus interviews and film/book/documentary reviews in the Loafing Lounge, and the best content from around the web in Bite Size.

London-based Jo also works as a freelance content provider for various media outlets including The Sunday Times, BBC Sport and Yahoo Sports UK.

You can contact Jo at jo@sportsliberated.com or follow her on Twitter at @sportsliberated and @jogunston. Sports Liberated is also on Instagram and a YouTube channel can be found at Sports Liberated TV.

30472067R00042

Printed in Poland
by Amazon Fulfillment
Poland Sp. z o.o., Wrocław